EMMANUEL JOSEPH

The Alchemy of Impact, Wealth, Power, and the Art of Redefining Tomorrow

Copyright © 2025 by Emmanuel Joseph

All rights reserved. No part of this publication may be reproduced, stored or transmitted in any form or by any means, electronic, mechanical, photocopying, recording, scanning, or otherwise without written permission from the publisher. It is illegal to copy this book, post it to a website, or distribute it by any other means without permission.

First edition

This book was professionally typeset on Reedsy.
Find out more at reedsy.com

Contents

1	Chapter 1: The Essence of Wealth	1
2	Chapter 2: The Power Paradigm	3
3	Chapter 3: The Art of Redefining Tomorrow	5
4	Chapter 4: Transformative Leadership	7
5	Chapter 5: The Economics of Impact	9
6	Chapter 6: The Ethics of Wealth and Power	11
7	Chapter 7: The Dynamics of Influence	13
8	Chapter 8: The Pursuit of Excellence	15
9	Chapter 9: The Role of Education	17
10	Chapter 10: Social Responsibility and Civic Engagement	19
11	Chapter 11: Building Resilient Communities	21
12	Chapter 12: The Power of Collaboration	23
13	Chapter 13: The Role of Technology	25
14	Chapter 14: The Future of Work	27
15	Chapter 15: The Power of Purpose	29
16	Chapter 16: The Intersection of Wealth and Power	31
17	Chapter 17: Crafting a Legacy of Impact	33

1

Chapter 1: The Essence of Wealth

In the heart of every civilization lies the pursuit of wealth. For centuries, humans have strived to amass resources that transcend mere survival. The essence of wealth is not limited to tangible assets but extends to knowledge, skills, and experiences that enrich one's life. Understanding wealth in its multifaceted form requires a shift in perception from monetary gain to holistic fulfillment. It is essential to recognize that true wealth encompasses financial stability, intellectual growth, emotional well-being, and social connections.

The accumulation of wealth often leads to a sense of security and freedom. With financial stability, individuals can pursue their passions, invest in their communities, and contribute to societal progress. However, wealth should not be hoarded for personal gain; it should be harnessed to create opportunities for others. The impact of wealth is magnified when it is used to uplift those in need, fostering a culture of generosity and collective prosperity.

In modern society, the digital age has revolutionized the way wealth is created and distributed. The advent of technology has democratized access to information and resources, enabling individuals from diverse backgrounds to achieve financial success. The rise of entrepreneurship, remote work, and digital currencies has redefined the landscape of wealth, creating new avenues for economic empowerment. Embracing these changes is crucial for navigating the complexities of the contemporary world.

Ultimately, the essence of wealth lies in its ability to transform lives and communities. It is a tool that, when wielded responsibly, can bring about positive change and redefine the future. By fostering a mindset of abundance and sharing, individuals can create a ripple effect that transcends generations, leaving a legacy of prosperity and progress.

2

Chapter 2: The Power Paradigm

Power, like wealth, is a force that shapes societies and influences human behavior. It is the ability to effect change, command respect, and drive innovation. The power paradigm is a complex interplay of authority, influence, and leadership. Understanding the dynamics of power requires an exploration of its sources, manifestations, and ethical implications.

Authority is a formal aspect of power, often conferred through positions of leadership or governance. However, true power extends beyond titles and ranks; it is rooted in the ability to inspire, motivate, and empower others. Influential individuals possess the charisma and vision to rally people around a common cause, creating a sense of unity and purpose. The power of influence is often more potent than formal authority, as it transcends organizational hierarchies and resonates on a personal level.

The ethical use of power is paramount in ensuring that it serves the greater good. Leaders must navigate the delicate balance between asserting control and fostering collaboration. Power can corrupt if wielded irresponsibly, leading to oppression, exploitation, and social injustice. Ethical leadership is grounded in principles of integrity, accountability, and empathy, ensuring that power is exercised with fairness and compassion.

The democratization of power in the digital age has empowered individuals and communities to challenge traditional structures and advocate for change.

Social media, activism, and grassroots movements have amplified the voices of marginalized groups, creating a more inclusive and equitable society. The power paradigm is shifting towards a more collaborative and participatory model, where individuals can influence decisions and drive social progress.

3

Chapter 3: The Art of Redefining Tomorrow

Redefining tomorrow is an art that requires vision, innovation, and resilience. It involves challenging the status quo, embracing change, and envisioning a future that transcends limitations. The art of redefining tomorrow is a dynamic process that demands creativity, adaptability, and a commitment to continuous improvement.

Vision is the cornerstone of redefinition. It is the ability to see beyond the present and imagine possibilities that others may overlook. Visionaries are trailblazers who challenge conventional wisdom and inspire others to dream big. They possess the foresight to anticipate trends, identify opportunities, and navigate uncertainties. Visionary leaders create a compelling narrative that galvanizes people towards a shared goal, fostering a sense of hope and purpose.

Innovation is the engine that drives redefinition. It is the process of transforming ideas into tangible outcomes that create value. Innovators are problem-solvers who leverage technology, creativity, and collaboration to address pressing challenges. They are unafraid to take risks, experiment, and learn from failures. The culture of innovation is characterized by a mindset of curiosity, openness, and resilience, enabling individuals and organizations to adapt to changing circumstances and seize emerging opportunities.

Resilience is the capacity to withstand adversity and bounce back stronger. It is the ability to navigate setbacks, learn from experiences, and persevere in the face of challenges. Resilient individuals and organizations possess the grit and determination to overcome obstacles, adapt to new realities, and continue on the path to progress. Resilience is fostered through a supportive environment, strong social networks, and a growth mindset that embraces change as an opportunity for growth.

The art of redefining tomorrow is a collective endeavor that requires collaboration, inclusivity, and a shared vision for a better future. It is about harnessing the collective potential of individuals and communities to create a more equitable, sustainable, and prosperous world. By embracing the principles of vision, innovation, and resilience, we can redefine tomorrow and shape a future that reflects our highest aspirations.

4

Chapter 4: Transformative Leadership

Transformative leadership is the cornerstone of creating impactful change. It involves guiding individuals and organizations towards a shared vision, fostering innovation, and nurturing a culture of growth. Transformative leaders inspire others by setting an example, demonstrating integrity, and exhibiting a genuine commitment to the collective good. They possess the ability to articulate a compelling vision that resonates with people and motivates them to strive for excellence.

Central to transformative leadership is the concept of servant leadership, where leaders prioritize the needs of their team members and stakeholders. This approach emphasizes empathy, active listening, and empowerment. Servant leaders build trust and foster a sense of belonging, encouraging collaboration and creativity. By placing the well-being of others at the forefront, transformative leaders cultivate an environment where individuals feel valued and motivated to contribute their best efforts.

Innovation is a driving force behind transformative leadership. Leaders who embrace change and encourage experimentation create a culture of continuous improvement. They empower their teams to think creatively, take calculated risks, and learn from failures. This mindset fosters resilience and adaptability, enabling organizations to navigate challenges and seize opportunities. Transformative leaders understand that innovation is not a one-time event but a continuous journey that requires persistence and dedication.

Ultimately, transformative leadership is about creating a lasting impact that extends beyond the immediate goals of an organization. It involves fostering a sense of purpose, aligning actions with values, and prioritizing the greater good. Transformative leaders leave a legacy of positive change, inspiring others to carry forward their vision and continue the work of redefining tomorrow.

5

Chapter 5: The Economics of Impact

The economics of impact explores the intersection of wealth, power, and societal change. It involves understanding how economic principles can be leveraged to create positive outcomes for individuals and communities. The traditional focus on profit maximization is shifting towards a more holistic approach that considers social and environmental impact. This paradigm shift reflects a growing recognition that economic success and societal well-being are interconnected.

Impact investing is a key component of the economics of impact. It involves directing capital towards ventures that generate both financial returns and positive social or environmental outcomes. Impact investors prioritize sustainability, inclusivity, and ethical practices, seeking to create value beyond monetary gains. This approach aligns financial interests with the greater good, fostering a more equitable and sustainable economy.

Corporate social responsibility (CSR) is another important aspect of the economics of impact. Businesses are increasingly recognizing their role in addressing societal challenges and contributing to the common good. CSR initiatives encompass a wide range of activities, from environmental sustainability and community engagement to ethical labor practices and philanthropy. By integrating CSR into their core operations, companies can enhance their reputation, build trust with stakeholders, and drive positive change.

The economics of impact also involves rethinking traditional economic models and metrics. Gross domestic product (GDP) and profit margins are no longer the sole indicators of success. New metrics, such as social return on investment (SROI) and well-being indices, provide a more comprehensive view of economic progress. These metrics take into account factors like quality of life, environmental sustainability, and social equity, offering a more nuanced understanding of economic impact.

6

Chapter 6: The Ethics of Wealth and Power

The ethics of wealth and power is a crucial consideration in the quest to redefine tomorrow. It involves examining the moral principles that guide the use of resources and influence. Ethical considerations are essential in ensuring that wealth and power are wielded responsibly and for the greater good. This chapter explores the ethical dilemmas and principles that shape the responsible use of wealth and power.

Integrity is a fundamental ethical principle that underpins the responsible use of wealth and power. It involves honesty, transparency, and accountability in actions and decisions. Individuals and organizations that operate with integrity build trust and credibility, fostering positive relationships with stakeholders. Ethical behavior is essential in preventing corruption, exploitation, and abuse of power, ensuring that wealth and power are used to create positive outcomes.

Equity is another important ethical consideration. It involves ensuring that resources and opportunities are distributed fairly, without discrimination or bias. Wealth and power should not be concentrated in the hands of a few but should be accessible to all. Ethical leaders and organizations prioritize diversity, inclusivity, and social justice, creating an environment where everyone has the opportunity to succeed.

The ethics of wealth and power also involve a commitment to social and environmental responsibility. Wealth and power should be used to address societal challenges, such as poverty, inequality, and environmental degradation. Ethical leaders and organizations prioritize sustainability, philanthropy, and community engagement, leveraging their resources and influence to create positive change. By aligning their actions with ethical principles, they contribute to a more just and sustainable world.

In conclusion, the ethics of wealth and power are essential in ensuring that these resources are used responsibly and for the greater good. By adhering to principles of integrity, equity, and social responsibility, individuals and organizations can wield their wealth and power to create a positive impact and redefine tomorrow.

7

Chapter 7: The Dynamics of Influence

Influence is a powerful force that shapes human behavior and societal change. It involves the ability to persuade, inspire, and motivate others. The dynamics of influence are complex and multifaceted, encompassing various forms of communication, relationships, and social structures. Understanding the dynamics of influence is essential for harnessing its potential to create positive change.

One of the key aspects of influence is communication. Effective communication involves not only conveying information but also building trust, empathy, and understanding. Influential individuals are skilled communicators who can articulate their vision, listen actively, and engage others in meaningful dialogue. They use storytelling, rhetoric, and emotional intelligence to connect with their audience and inspire action.

Relationships are another crucial component of influence. Building strong, authentic relationships is essential for establishing trust and credibility. Influential individuals invest in building rapport, showing genuine interest in others, and offering support and encouragement. They understand the importance of collaboration and leverage their networks to amplify their impact. By fostering positive relationships, they create a supportive environment that facilitates change.

Social structures also play a significant role in the dynamics of influence. Cultural norms, organizational hierarchies, and power dynamics shape how influence is exerted and received. Influential individuals navigate these structures with awareness and adaptability, understanding the nuances of social contexts. They leverage their positional and relational power to advocate for change and mobilize others. By understanding the dynamics of influence, they can strategically navigate social structures to create a positive impact.

In conclusion, the dynamics of influence are essential in shaping human behavior and societal change. Effective communication, authentic relationships, and an understanding of social structures are key components of influence. By harnessing the power of influence, individuals can inspire others, drive innovation, and create a positive impact on the world.

8

Chapter 8: The Pursuit of Excellence

The pursuit of excellence is a relentless journey that involves striving for the highest standards in all aspects of life. It is a mindset that embraces continuous improvement, self-discipline, and a commitment to achieving one's full potential. The pursuit of excellence is not about perfection but about progress and growth. It requires a willingness to learn, adapt, and persevere in the face of challenges.

Excellence begins with setting clear goals and defining a vision for success. Individuals who pursue excellence are driven by a sense of purpose and direction. They set ambitious yet achievable targets and develop a roadmap to guide their efforts. Goal-setting provides a sense of focus and motivation, helping individuals stay on track and measure their progress. By breaking down larger goals into smaller, manageable steps, they can celebrate incremental achievements and maintain momentum.

Self-discipline is a crucial component of the pursuit of excellence. It involves the ability to prioritize tasks, manage time effectively, and resist distractions. Self-disciplined individuals cultivate habits and routines that support their goals, ensuring that their actions align with their vision. They are proactive and take ownership of their success, recognizing that consistent effort and dedication are essential for achieving excellence. By developing self-discipline, individuals can navigate obstacles and stay committed to their path.

Continuous learning is another key aspect of the pursuit of excellence. Excellence is not a destination but a journey of ongoing growth and development. Individuals who pursue excellence are curious, open-minded, and eager to expand their knowledge and skills. They seek out opportunities for learning, whether through formal education, mentorship, or self-study. By embracing a growth mindset, they view challenges as opportunities for improvement and approach setbacks with resilience.

In conclusion, the pursuit of excellence is a lifelong commitment to growth, self-discipline, and continuous learning. It involves setting clear goals, developing self-discipline, and embracing a mindset of curiosity and resilience. By striving for excellence, individuals can achieve their full potential and make a meaningful impact on the world.

9

Chapter 9: The Role of Education

Education is a powerful tool that shapes individuals and societies, enabling them to navigate the complexities of the modern world. It provides the knowledge, skills, and values necessary for personal and professional growth. The role of education extends beyond the acquisition of information; it involves fostering critical thinking, creativity, and a lifelong love of learning.

One of the primary functions of education is to equip individuals with the foundational knowledge and skills needed for success. This includes literacy, numeracy, and digital literacy, as well as subject-specific knowledge in areas such as science, mathematics, and the arts. A strong educational foundation enables individuals to pursue further learning, engage in meaningful work, and contribute to society. Education also promotes social mobility, providing opportunities for individuals to improve their economic prospects and achieve their goals.

Critical thinking is a crucial component of education. It involves the ability to analyze information, evaluate evidence, and make informed decisions. Education encourages students to question assumptions, consider multiple perspectives, and engage in thoughtful reflection. By fostering critical thinking, education empowers individuals to navigate complex issues, solve problems, and make sound judgments. Critical thinking is essential for innovation, civic engagement, and ethical decision-making.

Creativity is another important aspect of education. It involves the ability to generate original ideas, think outside the box, and express oneself in unique ways. Education nurtures creativity by providing opportunities for exploration, experimentation, and collaboration. Creative individuals are adaptable, resourceful, and capable of finding innovative solutions to challenges. By fostering creativity, education prepares individuals to thrive in a rapidly changing world and contribute to the advancement of society.

In conclusion, education plays a vital role in shaping individuals and societies. It provides the foundational knowledge and skills needed for success, fosters critical thinking and creativity, and promotes lifelong learning. By investing in education, we can empower individuals to achieve their full potential and create a better future for all.

10

Chapter 10: Social Responsibility and Civic Engagement

Social responsibility and civic engagement are essential components of a thriving society. They involve a commitment to contributing to the common good and addressing social and environmental challenges. Socially responsible individuals and organizations prioritize ethical behavior, community involvement, and sustainability. Civic engagement involves active participation in the democratic process, advocacy, and volunteerism. Together, social responsibility and civic engagement create a culture of shared responsibility and collective action.

Ethical behavior is a cornerstone of social responsibility. It involves acting with integrity, fairness, and accountability in all aspects of life. Socially responsible individuals and organizations consider the impact of their actions on others and strive to minimize harm. They prioritize honesty, transparency, and respect for human rights. Ethical behavior fosters trust, credibility, and positive relationships, creating a foundation for social responsibility.

Community involvement is another important aspect of social responsibility. It involves actively engaging with and contributing to the well-being of local communities. This can take many forms, including volunteering, philanthropy, and supporting local initiatives. By building strong, supportive communities, individuals and organizations can create a sense of belonging and mutual support. Community involvement fosters social cohesion, resilience, and collective problem-solving.

Sustainability is a key consideration in social responsibility. It involves recognizing the interconnectedness of social, economic, and environmental systems and striving to create a balance that supports long-term well-being. Sustainable practices prioritize the responsible use of resources, environmental stewardship, and social equity. By adopting sustainable practices, individuals and organizations can contribute to a more equitable and resilient world.

Civic engagement is the active participation in the democratic process and efforts to address social issues. It involves voting, advocacy, and civic participation. By staying informed, voicing their opinions, and working together to solve problems, individuals can contribute to a more just and equitable society.

11

Chapter 11: Building Resilient Communities

Resilient communities are essential for fostering social, economic, and environmental well-being. They are characterized by their ability to adapt to challenges, bounce back from adversity, and thrive in the face of change. Building resilient communities involves creating strong social networks, promoting inclusivity, and fostering a sense of collective responsibility. It requires collaboration, resourcefulness, and a commitment to continuous improvement.

One of the key elements of resilient communities is strong social networks. These networks provide support, resources, and a sense of belonging. They enable individuals to come together, share knowledge, and coordinate efforts. Strong social networks foster trust, cooperation, and mutual aid, creating a foundation for resilience. By building and nurturing these networks, communities can enhance their capacity to respond to challenges and leverage their collective strengths.

Inclusivity is another important aspect of resilient communities. It involves ensuring that all individuals have access to resources, opportunities, and decision-making processes. Inclusive communities prioritize diversity, equity, and social justice, recognizing that everyone has a role to play in building resilience. By embracing inclusivity, communities can tap into a wide range of perspectives, skills, and experiences, enhancing their ability to innovate and adapt.

Collective responsibility is the shared commitment to the well-being of the community. It involves recognizing the interconnectedness of individuals and the impact of their actions on others. Collective responsibility encourages individuals to contribute to the common good, support one another, and take proactive measures to address challenges. By fostering a sense of collective responsibility, communities can create a culture of mutual support and accountability.

In conclusion, building resilient communities is essential for fostering social, economic, and environmental well-being. It involves creating strong social networks, promoting inclusivity, and fostering a sense of collective responsibility. By working together and leveraging their collective strengths, communities can navigate challenges, seize opportunities, and create a better future for all.

12

Chapter 12: The Power of Collaboration

Collaboration is a vital component in the pursuit of impactful change. It involves bringing together diverse perspectives, skills, and resources to achieve common goals. The power of collaboration lies in its ability to harness collective intelligence, foster innovation, and build stronger communities. By working together, individuals and organizations can amplify their efforts and create a greater impact than they could achieve alone.

Effective collaboration begins with open communication and trust. It is essential to create an environment where all voices are heard, and ideas are valued. Open communication fosters transparency, reduces misunderstandings, and encourages the sharing of knowledge and resources. Trust is the foundation of collaboration, enabling individuals to feel safe and supported as they work towards a common goal. Building trust requires honesty, integrity, and a commitment to follow through on commitments.

Diversity is a key strength in collaboration. Bringing together individuals with different backgrounds, experiences, and perspectives can lead to more innovative solutions and better decision-making. Diverse teams are more likely to challenge assumptions, identify blind spots, and develop creative approaches to problems. By embracing diversity, collaborative efforts can tap into a wider range of ideas and expertise, leading to more effective and sustainable outcomes.

Collaboration also involves a willingness to share power and resources. Successful collaboration requires a mindset of generosity and reciprocity, where individuals and organizations are willing to contribute their strengths and support others. This approach fosters a sense of collective responsibility and mutual benefit. By sharing resources and leveraging each other's strengths, collaborative efforts can achieve greater efficiency and impact.

In conclusion, the power of collaboration lies in its ability to harness collective intelligence, foster innovation, and build stronger communities. Effective collaboration requires open communication, trust, diversity, and a willingness to share power and resources. By working together, individuals and organizations can amplify their efforts and create a greater impact on the world.

13

Chapter 13: The Role of Technology

Technology plays a crucial role in shaping the future and driving impactful change. It has the potential to revolutionize industries, enhance communication, and improve the quality of life. The role of technology in redefining tomorrow involves leveraging its capabilities to address societal challenges, promote sustainability, and create new opportunities for growth and development.

One of the primary benefits of technology is its ability to enhance communication and connectivity. Digital platforms, social media, and communication tools have transformed the way people interact, share information, and collaborate. Technology has broken down geographical barriers, enabling individuals and organizations to connect and work together across distances. This increased connectivity fosters the exchange of ideas, resources, and expertise, facilitating innovation and progress.

Technology also plays a vital role in promoting sustainability. Advances in renewable energy, smart infrastructure, and resource-efficient technologies are helping to address environmental challenges and reduce the carbon footprint. Sustainable technologies promote the responsible use of resources, reduce waste, and minimize environmental impact. By integrating sustainability into technological innovation, we can create a more resilient and equitable future.

In addition, technology has the potential to create new opportunities for economic growth and development. The rise of the digital economy, automation, and artificial intelligence has transformed industries and created new avenues for entrepreneurship and employment. Technology has democratized access to information and resources, enabling individuals from diverse backgrounds to participate in the global economy. By embracing technological advancements, we can unlock new opportunities for economic empowerment and social progress.

In conclusion, technology plays a crucial role in shaping the future and driving impactful change. It enhances communication and connectivity, promotes sustainability, and creates new opportunities for growth and development. By leveraging the capabilities of technology, we can address societal challenges, foster innovation, and create a better future for all.

14

Chapter 14: The Future of Work

The future of work is undergoing a significant transformation, driven by technological advancements, globalization, and changing societal expectations. Understanding the trends and implications of this transformation is essential for navigating the evolving landscape of work. The future of work involves embracing flexibility, continuous learning, and a focus on well-being and inclusivity.

One of the key trends in the future of work is the rise of remote and flexible work arrangements. Technology has enabled individuals to work from anywhere, breaking down traditional office boundaries and creating new opportunities for work-life balance. Remote work offers flexibility in terms of location and schedule, allowing individuals to tailor their work environment to their needs. Organizations that embrace remote work can tap into a global talent pool, enhance productivity, and reduce overhead costs.

Continuous learning and upskilling are essential in the future of work. The rapid pace of technological change requires individuals to stay updated with new skills and knowledge. Lifelong learning is becoming a necessity, with individuals seeking opportunities for professional development, online courses, and skill-building programs. Organizations that prioritize continuous learning can foster a culture of growth and innovation, enabling employees to adapt to changing demands and stay competitive.

Well-being and inclusivity are also important considerations in the future of work. Organizations are increasingly recognizing the importance of supporting employees' mental, emotional, and physical well-being. This includes providing resources for stress management, promoting work-life balance, and creating a supportive work environment. Inclusivity involves ensuring that all employees have equal access to opportunities and are valued for their contributions. By prioritizing well-being and inclusivity, organizations can enhance employee satisfaction, retention, and overall performance.

In conclusion, the future of work is undergoing a significant transformation, driven by technological advancements and changing societal expectations. Embracing remote work, continuous learning, well-being, and inclusivity are key trends in this evolving landscape. By understanding and adapting to these trends, individuals and organizations can navigate the future of work and create a more flexible, innovative, and inclusive workforce.

15

Chapter 15: The Power of Purpose

The power of purpose is a driving force that motivates individuals and organizations to achieve meaningful and impactful goals. Purpose provides a sense of direction, inspiration, and fulfillment. It involves aligning actions with values and striving to make a positive difference in the world. The power of purpose is essential for creating a sense of meaning and driving lasting impact.

Having a clear sense of purpose begins with understanding one's values and passions. Purpose-driven individuals are guided by a deep-seated commitment to causes that resonate with them. They set goals that reflect their values and contribute to the greater good. This sense of purpose provides motivation and resilience, enabling individuals to overcome challenges and stay focused on their vision.

Purpose is also a powerful driver of organizational success. Purpose-driven organizations have a clear mission that goes beyond profit maximization. They prioritize social and environmental impact, creating value for stakeholders and society as a whole. Purpose-driven organizations attract and retain talent, build strong relationships with customers and partners, and drive innovation. By aligning their actions with their mission, these organizations create a positive and lasting impact.

The power of purpose also involves inspiring and empowering others. Purpose-driven leaders create a sense of shared vision and direction, motivating their teams to work towards common goals. They communicate the significance of their mission and create a culture of purpose, where everyone feels connected to the greater good. By fostering a sense of purpose, leaders can harness the collective potential of their teams and drive meaningful change.

In conclusion, the power of purpose is a driving force that motivates individuals and organizations to achieve meaningful and impactful goals. Purpose provides a sense of direction, inspiration, and fulfillment. By aligning actions with values and striving to make a positive difference, individuals and organizations can create a lasting impact and redefine tomorrow.

16

Chapter 16: The Intersection of Wealth and Power

The intersection of wealth and power is a complex and often controversial topic. It involves examining how financial resources and influence intersect to shape societal dynamics and impact individuals and communities. The relationship between wealth and power is multifaceted, with both positive and negative implications. Understanding this intersection is essential for navigating the complexities of modern society and creating a more equitable future.

Wealth can confer power by providing access to resources, opportunities, and influence. Financial resources enable individuals and organizations to invest in ventures, support causes, and shape public opinion. Wealthy individuals and entities often have the means to lobby for policy changes, fund political campaigns, and support philanthropic initiatives. This financial influence can drive positive change by addressing social and environmental challenges, promoting innovation, and supporting economic development.

However, the concentration of wealth and power can also lead to disparities and inequities. When wealth is concentrated in the hands of a few, it can create imbalances in access to opportunities, decision-making, and resources. This concentration of power can perpetuate social and economic inequalities, creating barriers for marginalized groups and limiting social mobility. Addressing these disparities requires a commitment to equity, inclusivity, and social justice.

The ethical use of wealth and power is crucial in ensuring that they contribute to the greater good. Ethical leaders and organizations prioritize transparency, accountability, and social responsibility. They recognize their influence and use it to advocate for positive change, support vulnerable communities, and promote sustainable practices. By aligning their actions with ethical principles, they can create a more just and equitable society.

In conclusion, the intersection of wealth and power is a complex and multifaceted topic with both positive and negative implications. Understanding this intersection is essential for navigating modern society and creating a more equitable future. By prioritizing ethical use, equity, and social responsibility, individuals and organizations can harness the potential of wealth and power to drive positive change.

17

Chapter 17: Crafting a Legacy of Impact

Crafting a legacy of impact involves creating a lasting, positive influence that extends beyond one's lifetime. It is about leaving a mark on the world that reflects one's values, vision, and contributions. A legacy of impact is built through intentional actions, meaningful relationships, and a commitment to creating a better future. This chapter explores the principles and strategies for crafting a legacy of impact.

Intentionality is a key principle in crafting a legacy of impact. It involves setting clear goals, defining a vision, and aligning actions with values. Intentional individuals and organizations are purposeful in their efforts to create positive change. They prioritize long-term impact over short-term gains, focusing on initiatives that have a lasting effect. By being intentional, they can ensure that their contributions are meaningful and aligned with their mission.

Relationships play a crucial role in crafting a legacy of impact. Building strong, authentic relationships with individuals, communities, and organizations creates a foundation for lasting influence. Relationships based on trust, respect, and collaboration enable individuals to mobilize support, amplify their efforts, and create a ripple effect of positive change. By investing in meaningful relationships, individuals can extend their impact and create a network of support for their legacy.

A commitment to continuous improvement is essential in crafting a legacy of impact. It involves a willingness to learn, adapt, and evolve over time. Individuals and organizations that are committed to growth and development are better equipped to navigate challenges and seize opportunities. They seek feedback, reflect on their experiences, and strive to improve their efforts. By embracing a mindset of continuous improvement, they can enhance their impact and create a more meaningful legacy.

In conclusion, crafting a legacy of impact involves intentional actions, meaningful relationships, and a commitment to continuous improvement. By setting clear goals, building strong relationships, and prioritizing long-term impact, individuals and organizations can create a lasting, positive influence on the world. A legacy of impact reflects one's values and vision, leaving a mark that transcends time and inspires future generations.

The Alchemy of Impact: Wealth, Power, and the Art of Redefining Tomorrow

In a world where the dynamics of wealth and power shape our lives and societies, "The Alchemy of Impact" delves into the intricate interplay of these forces and explores how they can be harnessed to create a better future. This thought-provoking book offers a fresh perspective on the essence of wealth, the power paradigm, and the art of redefining tomorrow.

Through 17 insightful chapters, the book examines transformative leadership, the economics of impact, the ethics of wealth and power, and the role of education and technology in shaping the future. It emphasizes the importance of social responsibility, civic engagement, and building resilient communities. Readers will discover the power of collaboration, the pursuit of excellence, and the significance of purpose in driving meaningful change.

"The Alchemy of Impact" is a compelling guide for individuals and organizations seeking to navigate the complexities of modern society and leave a lasting legacy of positive influence. With a focus on ethical behavior, inclusivity, and continuous improvement, this book provides valuable insights and practical strategies for creating a more equitable, sustainable, and prosperous world.

www.ingramcontent.com/pod-product-compliance
Lightning Source LLC
LaVergne TN
LVHW020458080526
838202LV00057B/6022